It Came to My Ear

It Came to My Ear

Malinda Williams

Rev. date: 09/05/2018

To order additional copies of this book, contact:
Xlibris
1-888-795-4274
www.Xlibris.com
Orders@Xlibris.com
783461

Dedication

To my dear children Michael, Isaiah, and Melaysha. I say to you "don't just see the dream but be the dream" to all of you who had a listening ear to these quotes. To Mom and all of my siblings, A special thanks to Dr. Terrence Parris and his wife who encouraged me and prophesied the manifestation of this book.

To my dad David Williams (1953-2018) who will never read this book but heard many of these quotes. A gracious thanks to Richard Solis for believing in me and said I sound like I'm ready to write this book, and the entire team of Xlibris for their patience and tedious work on this book.

"Shattered glasses can become whole mirrors"- An individual can be destroyed for a period of time in their lives but they can overcome and be whole again.

"The heart forgives but the mind records"-
you can forgive a person but you will
always remember what they have done.

"Never wake a silent lion"- If you know someone
is angry with you do not bother them...

"Some situations need to sleep"
sometimes you need to let things rest
and it will work out on it's own.

"What good is a fit body witth a crazy mind?- it makes no sense to be physically well and have an unhealthy mind... for the mind controls the body...

"Pictures tell lies and truths"- There are messages in them you just have to see what is being revealed.

"Fight with me not against me"

"The evil that you do will return to you"

"Don't confuse a soul with a soulmate" - You think an individual is God sent but they're actually a soul you must win.

"A bleeding heart can still love" You may have a broken heart but love still exist within you...

"He chose a knife over his wife"- A man can
be deceived and leave his family for a snake.

"It's better to be than to look like" - People may appear to be something but who they really are will be revealed.

"Sometimes you have to be the listener and not the talker"- There are times when people don't need your advice just let them vent.

"Joining people together that don't agree is like forcing a marriage" If you're not on the same page it can't work

"People leave physically but there is still heart relations"- You can move on in life and still love a person...

"Words can hurt or heal be careful what you say"

"Humans surprise themselves"! - You never
know what's in you until it comes out.

"Answer what your asked and give no more"

"The wisdom remains after the extraction" you may have lost something but you've learned a lesson...

"A haughty man is noticed but a
humble man is respected"

"There is a difference between love and lust" - love last but lust gets lost...

"People are like puzzles they
need to be put together"

"Never throw away treasure and pick up trash"- If you have good don't replace it with something that has no value...

"The mind have many journeys
depending on it's state"

"Love is not blind it can be seen by people"

"Remove the weeds before you plant" - before you
start something new get rid of the old things...

"Be your own company"

"Some confrontations is necessary for healing"
- you will never be well until you face the issue

"A pie must be whole before it's divided" - you can't give of yourself if you're not complete...

"True friends don't conceal but they reveal" - you shouldn't be the only one sharing...

"Opportunity is a doorknob
waiting for you to turn it"-

"God can make an agitator become a mediator" - the very one that caused the trouble may have to bring unity...

"Words are not like food you
can't swallow them back"

"A transformed man is better than a broken one"

"To many opinions are not good" -wrong advice
is like posion be mindful of who you talk to.

"Silence is a response"

"Never make a decision in wrath"- emotions
can cause you to self destruct!

"Negative thoughts are like viruses delete them"

"It's not that people have changed they
were always that way you couldn't see"

"A princess is to a father but a
Queen is for the husband"

"If you don't divorce your past you
can't marry your future"

"Forgive quickly so the cancer doesn't grow"

"A chapter has to close for a new book to be written" - if you dwell on your past the future is hindered...

"Don't chase after something that left you"

"Returning to your past is like going
back to the bee that stung you"

"The greatest hypocrite is to tell someone
to do something you don't do"

"You can't decide how you want to hear the truth"

"Some wisdom is not to be shared"

"Don't let the devil take a piece of your peace"

"Anything free is a secret gain"

"You can't replace waste once it's flushed"

"God blesses the good and the evil"

"Some dreams are lieing thoughts" if
you think about it you'll dream it...

"My legacy is the mark i leave on people"

"It hurts to let go but it hurts more holding on"

"A foolish man leave the door open but a
wise man sees opportunity and shuts it"

"When you do things to not be
alone you'll end up alone"

"When people think they are hurting
you they are actually helping you"

"Rebounds are quick fix for sudden disasters"

"The truth has a way of surfacing don't dive for it"

"Angels are ordinary people perceived
as friendly strangers"

"Don't publish before it's time"

"The book with no cover is truth"- when you
have nothing to hide everything is open...

"Don't look for it love knows how to find you"

"An unforgiving heart is like a clogged artery"

"A bandage cover wounds but don't heal them"

"Talk less and observe more"

"Your response determines your strengths and weaknesses" - you tell others who you are...

"You can't see a persons heart but it
speaks through their mouth"

"Misery need a crowd but peace can walk alone"

"The grave can only hold you
not your possessions"

"Leaders don't hang with the
crowd they lead them"

"Yesterday is deceased" - do not entertain
it because it no longer exist...

"People are for reasons and seasons"- they have serve their purpose and it's time for them to go.

"Tears are not weakness but they're strength"

"Sometimes the truth sounds like a lie"

"You steer the wheel to your life"

"It should never be a struggle being you"

CPSIA information can be obtained
at www.ICGtesting.com
Printed in the USA
BVHW07s0248181018
530448BV00002B/682/P